NATURAL HOME STYLE

NATURAL HOME STYLE

Using Simple Materials, Plantings and Sunlight

By Mirko Mejetta and Simonetta Spada
Translated by Meg Shore

Whitney Library of Design
An imprint of Watson-Guptill Publications, New York

First published in the United States and
Canada by the Whitney Library of Design,
an imprint of Watson-Guptill Publications,
1515 Broadway, New York, N.Y. 10036

Library of Congress Catalog Card Number:
85-50930 ISBN 0-8230-7387-4

Copyright © Gruppo Editoriale Electa,
Milan 1985

Translation copyright © 1985 by Whitney
Library of Design

Printed by Fantonigrafica, Venice/Italy,
a company of Gruppo Editoriale Electa.
First printing 1985.

HOUSES AND LANDSCAPES

VACATION HOMES

LIGHT AND GREEN SPACES IN THE CITY

NATURAL MATERIALS

GLASS HOUSES AND ALTERNATE ENERGY

Managing Editor
Dorothea Balluff

Text
Mirko Mejetta

Art Director/Layout
Simonetta Spada

Photos by:
Sergio Anelli (pp. 64, 72, 102)
Gabriele Basilico (pp. 22, 74)
Reiner and Anja Blunck (pp. 10, 14, 50, 108, 112, 116)
Brecht-Einzig Ltd (pp. 120, 122)
Fabio Cianchetti (p. 60)
Roberto Collovà (p. 16)
Giovanna Dal Magro (p. 28)
Gilles De Chabanneix (p. 68)
Donato D'Urbino and Roberta Frateschi (p. 32)
Giacomo Giannini (p. 26)
Lars Hallen and Lidia Sundelius (pp. 30, 46, 52, 56)
Giancarlo Iliprandi (p. 36)
Massimo Listri (p. 82)
Nino Lo Duca (p. 86)
Bruno Mio (p. 92)
Luciana Mulas (p. 98)
Per Nagel (p. 42)
Richard Payne (p. 38)
Paolo Pelli (p. 114)
Matteo Piazza (p. 62)
Bent Rej (p. 48)
Studio Tommasi (p. 78)
Rüdiger Zeitz (p. 106)

Editor for Whitney Library of Design
Stephen A. Kliment

"Besides this, I had my country seat, and I had now a tolerable plantation there also. For first, I had my little bower, as I called it, which I kept in repair. That is to say, I kept the hedge which circled it in, constantly fitted up to its usual height, the ladder standing always in the inside. I kept the trees, which at first were no more than my stakes, but were now grown very firm and tall. I kept them always so cut that they might spread and grow thick and wild, and make the more agreeable shade, which they did effectually to my mind. In the middle of this I had my tent always standing, being a piece of a sail spread over poles set up for that purpose, and which never wanted any repair or renewing. And under this I had made me a squab, or couch, with the skins of the creatures I had killed and with other soft things, and a blanket laid on them such as belonged to our seabedding, which I had saved, and a great watch coat to cover me. And here, whenever I had occasion to be absent from my chief seat, I took up my country habitation.
Adjoining to this I had my enclosures for my cattle, that is to say, my goats. And as I had taken an inconceivable deal of pains to fence and enclose this ground, so I was so uneasy to see it kept entire, lest the goats should break through, and I never left off till with infinite labour I had struck the outside of the hedge so full of small stakes, and so near to one another, that it was rather a pale than a hedge, and there was scarce room to put a hand through between them, which afterwards, when those stakes grew, as they all did in the next rainy season, made the enclosure strong, like a wall, indeed stronger than any wall." (From *Robinson Crusoe* by Daniel Defoe).

Gentlemen used to travel to the countryside to visit their land holdings. They arrived in their dusty carriages and recuperated from their journeys in the cool quiet of their villas. Today's bourgeois custom of the country house, chalet, or cottage, continues that aristocratic tradition in scaled down fashion. As we travel the countryside, choosing alternative routes or adventurous paths, we often come upon abandoned farmhouses, empty dairies, small houses, already transformed into Piranesian ruins, covered with vines and berry bushes. In more poetic terms, we look with sympathetic eyes upon a personalized architecture, the material culture, one of the basic forms through which a popular vernacular is being expressed. At the same time, we share in the growing awareness and sensitivity to ecological and environmental problems — an awareness often manifested as a dissatisfaction with urban life and a renewed interest in craftsmanship and building by hand. The results are lively and stimulating testimony to the search for new life styles in both city and country.

HOUSES AND LANDSCAPES

HOUSE IN THE WOODS

This house emerges from a small clearing surrounded by woods, like a little enchanted castle or a witch's gingerbread house. A single family villa, it was built in a natural park area outside of Graz, Austria, by architects Michael Szyszkowitz and Karla Kowalski. Forms and materials interact in a play of concavities and convexities: the volumes, bared and separated along the perimeter of the plan, are subtly integrated through a close interweaving of wood, glass, brick, and iron.

The house is arranged on three levels: a common living area on the ground floor; individual bedrooms on the second floor; spaces for work and recreation on the top floor beneath the roof. The basement level provides mechanical services and storage. The two half-barrel vaults clad in vertical wood staves at opposite ends of the roof come together in a central, double-glazed peaked roof which also functions as a solar collector. Here, the many articulated spaces of the construction converge. The house opens up along this southern façade with terraces and large windows, protected and enhanced by screens, rain gutters, cantilevers, and shades — all in a dramatic sequence of decorative details.

The north wall is almost entirely closed off, and the roof slopes down to meet the central area of the structure.

The main entrance leads into the living area. A gallery onto which the bedrooms open overlooks the entry area. The floor is laid out on the diagonal, with squares of beech wood and strips of oak. The dining and living areas are contained in niches along the two sides of the central atrium. The well defined and decorated volume of the chimney functions as a plastic core around which a seating area is arranged. The carefully chosen, refined furnishings mesh nicely with both the design scheme and the various fixtures, which are emphasized by means of color.

Left: The north façade is closed. The roof creates a saddle-shaped connection between the two vaults; cut out of the central section, it slopes downward. The overall feeling is one of delight. The construction mixes varied materials in a playful, expressive interpretation of vernacular language: bricks, plaster, wood, iron, glass, white door and window frames.

Right: The south façade is sunny and open, with terraces and windows. The roof of the central element functions as a solar collector. The vaults are clad in vertical wood staves. The house is organized on three levels: the common living area on the ground floor; individual bedrooms on the first floor; work and recreation areas on the top floor beneath the roof.

Left: Great attention has been given to decorative details: the quasi-portico, protruding gutters, and window frames are reminiscent of the design tradition of the Viennese Secession.

Below: The portico-like shape along the south façade delineates a wood brise-soleil, which culminates in the overhang of the rain gutters.

Right: The small doorway is reminiscent of the Viennese tradition. The wall is plastered in terracotta tones. Window and door frames are white and flame red. The exterior walls also have areas covered in solid and carved wood.

Below: The glass-roofed gallery onto which open the second floor bedrooms. The design throughout conveys a sense of affection and an attention to detail; it corresponds to an aristocratic and civilized idea of living, with a fortunate ability to weave forms and construction elements into an imaginary castle in miniature.

Left: Dining and living room areas are contained in niches off the central atrium. The fireplace/chimney molds the space and divides the area.

Below: From the south façade one enters the living area, open above to the bedroom gallery. The floor, laid out diagonally, is made up of beech wood squares and oak strips.

CHALET ON A LAKE

A framework of larch wood covered by the narrow triangle of the roof: this chalet is suspended above the magical lake-filled landscape in the Carinthia section of Austria. The project, by architect Manfred Kovatsch, revives building elements typical of the region, reinventing in vertical fashion the familiar forms of the Alpine hut: open spaces, hay lofts, narrow stairs, small openings, the use of wood throughout. Glass, plexiglas, exposed fixtures, and the ordered arrangement of building elements all express the modern spirit behind the concept and design. The subtle wood structure, with its vanes, planks, trusses, windbreaks, and tie beams, is seen in the landscape in profoundly different ways, depending upon one's viewing position. Seen from above, the structure appears perfectly integrated into the landscape, lying against the slopes of the mountain. From below, looking up from the shores of the lake, it appears to be hovering, free against the sky, subtle and elegant.

The small photos, above: The subtle lines of the house against the landscape, as seen from the lake shore (left) and from above (right).

Upper right: The terrace/lookout juts out over the corner of the structure.

Right: Continuity between the living room and the terrace is by means of the double window wall. The furnishings are limited to simple canvas chairs and a cylindrical heater.

Opposite: The interior spaces are organized vertically. The living room is overlooked by the kitchen/dining area with its table and benches along the edge of the balcony. A short flight of steps passes above the counter area, leading to the night zone, which is furnished rather bizarrely, with bathroom fixtures in open view.

BETWEEN AN OLIVE GROVE AND THE SEA

This small house was built by architects Pasquale Culotta and Giuseppe Leone in an olive grove a short distance from the residential center of Cefalù (on the north coast of Sicily). The house stretches out into the landscape, organized by means of exterior spaces (patios, terraces, stairs, pergolas) more than by protected, covered areas.

The interior nucleus of the building consists of a volume of about 900 sq. ft. (85 sq. m.) which contains the living room, the kitchen area, two bedrooms, and the bathroom. The patios, the pergola, the outdoor cooking area, and the small outbuildings for storage and laundry — all enclosed and protected by an outer wall — make up a an area of 2100 sq. ft. (200 sq. m.), which surrounds the principal spaces of the living zone and provides that area with a continuous sense of air and a view to the outside.

One approaches the house through a long pergola made of fir wood strips gently set within the olive grove. The trellis casts shadows in rhythmic bands on the light blue gravel, recalling the interior streets of the casbahs of Marrakesh or Tunis. Façade openings are framed in the traditional blue of the area. On one side a steep stairway leads to the roof terrace and cistern. The choice of materials and the definition of the building elements evoke the Arab architecture of north African market cities. The interior spaces of the house are pared down and basic. Each element is designed with

Right: The sky, the olive grove, and a tree, framed within the patio of this house in Cefalù. Façade openings are framed in blue plaster and shuttered off to keep out the flies, as in Moroccan villages. The planes and volumes intersect quietly against the calm blue sky. The trellis of wood beams rests on the enclosing wall and is set into a deep opening in the wall. Behind the shutters lies the large window of the bedroom.

simplicity and a maximum use of space in mind. A small wood balcony supported by red iron beams overlooks the living room. The design encourages a free, continuous use of the living spaces. The clear line of a staircase cut out of the double wood panelling links the loft with the night zone. A bedroom is separated from the corridor by a wall constructed out of modular elements, wedged under the stairs. Each room faces onto its own private patio. This Mediterranean architecture expresses itself in terms of the exterior design through use of natural elements, which are incorporated into a sensitive and versatile whole.

Le Corbusier wrote: "Architecture is the knowledgeable, correct, and magnificent play of volume assembled in daylight." The waters of the Mediterranean have always reflected architecture that is tender and childlike, brightly colored and solar — an architecture that reflects the history, climate, and legends of the area. Mediterranean architecture is the result of an intricate and expressive interaction between classical culture and the Arab world, between full sunlight and the mysteries of shadow, incised in a geometrical web of Islamic decoration.

Upper right: The stairway connecting the bedrooms to the loft which overlooks the living room. The design encourages free and continuous use of the living area. Above, the wood loft wall is supported by red iron beams. On the left, two light switches of an industrial design; lighting fixtures throughout the house are simple and functional.

Right: The storage wall separating a bedroom from the corridor. The interior spaces are extremely restrained. Each element is designed with an eye to simplicity and the maximum use of space.

Below: The cooking area in the living room. The horizontal window above the counter is filled with light from the olive grove.

Above: The house extends outward; each bedroom opens onto its own private patio.

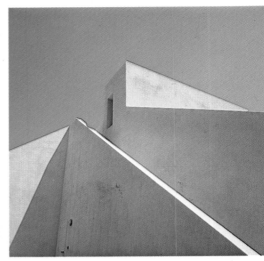

Upper left: The long pergola made of fir wood stretches beyond the house, connecting it to the surrounding landscape.

Upper right: The terrace with the silhouetted form of the cistern.

Right: The steep exterior staircase leading to the roof.

Opposite: A view down the pergola. The shadows cast by the roof recall the interior streets of north African cities. In the foreground, the outdoor kitchen counter, with the bread oven in the back. On the right, the edge of the long enclosing wall.

PALACE IN POSITANO

A steep succession of houses are stacked one upon the other along the terraced hillside that overlooks the magnificent basin. Positano was always the chosen vacation spot of the Neapolitan nobility. Here, they built large, shady palaces, like this one built in the 18th century, that passed directly from the Derossi family to Gioacchino Murat.

On the exterior the palace remains closed and severe, wedged into the hill that rises straight up from the sea. It is a jumbled, vertical collage of minute pieces: white longitudinal arches, elementary stone volumes, pink, yellow, and Pompeian red plaster, green and blue shutters, flowering pergolas and walls.

The interior of the palace, however, is a stately and convivial space, opening onto a courtyard. A portico with longitudinal arches forms a foundation which supports a continuous balcony. Above, two floors are framed by pilasters and are enclosed by the double elliptical openings of the attic level. An enormous bougainvillea climbs up from the garden, covering the second floor railings.

The interior spaces have been reorganized and furnished by architect Gennaro Passerotti. The floor of the entrance atrium is covered in squares of white and black marble. All exterior window frames have been repainted ochre and white; the interior doors have been left in their natural wood.

In the kitchen, to the sides of the monumental pediment, beautiful built-in, decorated pieces of furniture lie against the tiled walls, facing the large glass table.

Above: The façade of the interior courtyard. The breakfast tables are Antonia Astori's "Astragalo" (designed for Driade); the "Delfina" chairs are by Enzo Mari (also for Driade).

Left: Two views of the entrance atrium from the interior courtyard looking toward the stairwell. The floors are covered in squares of white and black marble.

Right: A view of Positano showing the steep way of houses stacked one on top of the other along the terraced hillside, overlooking the splendid basin. This is perhaps the most typical example of unity of architecture and site along the Mediterranean coast.

Following page: The kitchen with its lovely pediment. The polychrome built-in furniture is original. The "Cubino" table and "Delfina" chairs are by Enzo Mari for Driade.

23

ON AN ISLAND

This house by Sandra Severi and Pucci Corbetta overlooks the bay of Stintino in Sardinia, amid the splendid landscape of sea, wind, rocks, and dry, harsh vegetation. The building seems to be a deliberate reinterpretation of the Roman patio house, where the central space is monumental, leaving the task of closure and protection to the clear, elementary volumes of the living area. Here, the formality scheme has dissolved on one side of the outer wall, revealing the intimate structure of the interior architecture — a decision that allows the landscape to flow freely into the spaces and volumes and life of the building.

The rooms appear silhouetted against the supporting stone wall. Two end blocks frame the shielded core of the house. The patio is defined by a forest of subtle metal columns which support the roof. The center of the roof is open to the sky and overlooks the patio's central grassy area. During the summer, the open roof is closed over with large sheets or white stretched canvas.

Joining the living room and courtyard, the large window creates a dramatic relationship between interior and exterior, making the landscape an active element in the overall scheme.

Right: The open patio, with its sequence of subtle columns, encloses a small rectangle of green within the boundaries of the house.

Upper right: From the sea, this villa in Stintino, Sardinia, appears as two stone volumes, connected by the subtle framework of the colonnade. Carved out of the surrounding rock, the house stretches out as a delicate line between sky and sea, amid the dry vegetation of the bay.

Opposite: a view of the living room. The large window wall between the patio and living room creates a soft, dreamlike relationship between interior and exterior.

SHELTERED FROM THE WIND

This house, designed by architect Angelo Cortesi for his family and himself, consists of white volumes which act as wind shelters. The house is situated at the extreme southern point of Sardinia. The two simple volumes, the day house and the night house, are protected by the double pitched roof, like a traditional fisherman's house with its crenelations of terracotta tiles. The front of the house is defined by two deep porches from which the interior spaces extend. Within, the furnishings have been built in: tables, benches, containers — utterly simple — made from plastered masonry. There are only a few indispensable objects. The house is articulated by diffused sunlight, reflecting from the white surfaces, and the contrasting clear shadows created by the simple geometry of planes and volumes. An absence of detail and applied finish underscores the deliberately restrained vocabulary. Built in 1980 with great simplicity and economy, the house manages to accommodate, within just 800 sq. ft. (75 sq. m.), a living room, kitchen, three bedrooms, and two bathrooms.

Above: The house, built on the extreme southern point of Sardinia, consists of two simple adjacent volumes, defined by large open porches on both façades.

Right: The entrance porch to the day zone. These exterior spaces have tiled floors and built in furniture, and thus extend the house's usable space outdoors.

Right: A view from the living room toward the kitchen. The furnishings are fixed masonry elements, covered in light, shiny tiles, as are the floors.

Below: At one end of the house the long balcony/landing extends outward to form an outdoor dining terrace, shielded by a wooden framework.

COUNTRY STREET FRONT

This house, built by architect Jørgen Møller for an executive of *Form og Farve* (Copenhagen's most sophisticated store for housewares and furnishings), is situated on a hillside in the Danish countryside, along one of the loveliest residential streets in all of Europe. The structure is a combination of masonry and reinforced concrete and supports a traditional wood-beamed roof which is covered with wood planks on the interior and sheets of prefabricated panels on the exterior. On the south side, looking toward the hillside, large windows open onto a cantilevered balcony with planked floors and tubular metal railings. Facing north, small irregular openings (an expression of the spaces within) are cut out of the white plastered walls. The window frames are made of wood; some are filled with fixed panes.

The borderline between interior and exterior space is minimized; the space is used to its utmost. The interior spaces are quite varied; the living room is wood and white plaster with a chimney carved out of a large central pier. The house unfolds, one space after another, in a light filled perspective. Along the outer walls, vertical masonry partitions frame a series of niches in which various objects are set: the red door, the ceiling lamp, the curved wood chair. The entire building reflects a discreet technical design vocabulary.

Opposite, lower left: The long, planked balcony/landing on the south façade, facing onto the steep slope of the hillside, filled with tall trees.

Opposite, lower right: Exterior niches, formed by vertical masonry partitions, frame objects and furnishings. Shown here are the red door and two fixed windows looking out toward the access ramp to the cellar.

Right: The sizes of the windows vary according to the space and the amount of light required. Objects are treated with great care and affection and raised to the status of decorative elements in the design.

Below: The large chimney carved out of the central pier, beneath the ridge of the roof. The white plaster abuts sheets of wood paneling.

A HOUSE AND A BOAT

De Pas, D'Urbino, and Lomazzi are all expert sailors, solid craftsmen, and experienced architects with a sense of irony. These two projects show the restoration of an antique sailboat and a house, designed in collaboration with Vittorio Bozzoli, along the shores of Lake Como. These are two very different projects, but both come alive with the element of water – one floating upon it, the other overlooking it.

The boat was a Ligurian trading vessel; the architects have focused on the reorganization and furnishing of the hold area. Where cheeses and demijohns of wine were once stored, guests can now make themselves comfortable in a unique environment, finished with simple and harmonious means. The house is built on elevated piers in the center of a broad clearing. The ground floor accommodates boats and boating supplies which surround the entrance block. The linear façade is punctuated by a loggia with a classic openwork parapet. The walls are made of exposed cement block; the roof is covered in prefabricated panels.

Above: The *Felice Manin,* perfectly restored and under sail. The boat was built toward the end of the last century.

Center: Detail of the mast. Original materials have been used to faithfully restore the boat.

Left: A view of the furnished hold. The base of the large mast, anchored by horizontal bands of painted metal, passes through the center of the ceiling.

Left: The house presents a geometrical, elementary figure in the landscape by means of the grillwork of the structural scheme; the piers; the plane of the loggia onto which the rooms face. The walls are made of square concrete blocks.

Above: A classic Corbusian motif, seen in the grillwork of the interior stairway parapet.

Left: The interior spaces, achieved with great naturalness, face out toward the vertical divisions of the loggia, overlooking the surrounding landscape which forms a backdrop for the ample windows.

33

VACATION HOMES

INDOOR LEMON GARDEN

During the 19th century this building held a spinning mill and an installation for breeding silkworms. In 1911 the upper story was transformed into an indoor lemon garden, and the rest into a greenhouse. Facing onto a park on the shores of Lago Maggiore, this splendid piece of architecture has now become a residential dwelling. Architects Rosanna Monzini and Giulio Crespi have left organization of the space unaltered, for the most part. The extremely high windows still illuminate the enormous upper room, which is now a living room of monumental proportion. The large space has larchwood floors and white plaster walls; at one end is a large billiard table and two tripod chairs next to a telescope. At the other end is a conversation nook with two simple sofas arranged on a warm-colored carpet. Behind the sofas, the wooden stairway rises up to the loft area, a more protected and enclosed space. Beneath the loft lies the dining area, nestled against a subtle white wall, the plane of which is broken by the door opening.

Above: The indoor lemon garden, built during the last century, is adjacent to a large meadow overlooking the lake.

Center: The dining area furnished with both mass-produced and period pieces. The Saarinen table is manufactured by Knoll International.

Left: View of the living room from the billiard table, looking toward the loft. The large arched windows can be shaded by vertically sliding curtains.

Right: From the loft one can take in the entire space of the former indoor lemon garden. Period pieces are elegantly integrated with the refined, simple furnishings.

TEXAN VILLA

Gwathmey Siegel and Associates designed the renovation and reorganization of the interior of this villa in Texas which was built in various stages, beginning in the 1950s. The new additions and the outbuildings are organized around the original volume of the sloping roof. The new façade is defined by light elements, such as the exterior beam which virtually connects the curve of the patio with the entrance and the outdoor tool shed.
The interior spaces are precisely arranged around certain functional locations (stair, services), freeing up large wall areas to interact with the exterior landscape, which seems to pour in through the large windows.
A corner of the living room is fitted with a storage area, wedged beneath the stairs which lead to the rooms above. The dining room is dominated by a bright contemporary painting. The floor of the billiard room – and the living area – is covered with a heavy carpet. A steep airplane-style flight of stairs leads from this area up to a corner of the secluded, silent study.

Above: The study in the loft area, furnished with a curved table that fits into the volume of the supporting wall.

Upper right: Centerpiece for the dining room is a vivid contemporary painting. The table and chairs are by Knoll International.

Right: A corner of the living room has a storage wall wedged beneath the staircase. The armchairs are Le Corbusier's LC1, manufactured by Cassina.

Opposite: A flight of airplane stairs leads from the billiard room to the loft area.

Opposite, above: The new façade is defined by light elements like the exterior beam and the cylindrical pink unit which shields the patio.

Opposite, below: A view of the entrance and the walkway which leads past the pool to the house.

Above: Another view of the pool which has been dug out of the patio. In the background is the entrance area with its square-gridded metal gate. Above, the blue exterior beam.

SMALL HOUSE IN DENMARK

Set within dense woods, this small Danish house is a vacation and weekend family refuge. Architect Bertel Udsen opted for a compact solution, concentrating on a rectangular block for the well-defined living zone and an alcove/niche for the night zone. The living room is a single space, well organized into groupings which relate harmoniously to the storage wall containing all the kitchen fixtures. Off the living room is a dressing room which leads to a bathroom.

The north side of the house is protected by a thick brick wall painted with white enamel. This wall enters the house in the form of the chimney; it extends outside where it shields a wood platform raised up on heavy logs — a sort of terrace/patio. On the other side of the living room the platform leads to a second, separate area which holds two guest bedrooms.

The exterior walls are covered in curved asbestos sheets or planks of wood treated with waterproof paint — black for the walls, red for the door and window frames.

In the garden that surrounds the house, a separate structure is used as a tool shed. The materials employed — lacquered wood and painted brick — immediately identify it as belonging to the rest of the complex.

Equally simple materials are used in the house's interior: sisal rugs on the floors, natural woods for furniture and paneling, painted brick on the outer walls, canvas on the dividing walls.

The sloping roof is protected on the inside by a surface of natural wood staves which extend down alongside the chimney to form the back wall of a loft, which is reached by a ladder.

The furnishing, carefully chosen mass-produced pieces, are extremely simple, leaving the definition of the space to the building materials themselves.

Right: this small vacation/weekend house is in the midst of a Danish forest. The elevated platform acts to separate the two main building areas from the sun porch.

Opposite, above: The day zone seen from the entrance on the platform. In the foreground, the chimney and loft area take advantage of the slope of the roof. In the background is the storage wall of the kitchen. To the right, behind the chimney, lie the dressing room and bathroom.

Opposite, below: The reverse view of the previous image. In the foreground, the conversation area and then the large window wall of the entrance. On the left, the thick outer wall of painted brick which extends along the platform and then into the other block of the house which contains guest bedrooms. In the background, the glass doors with red frames.

Below: The brick fireplace corner is next to a glass opening in the outer wall. In the foreground is an old cast iron stove.

OWNER-BUILT HOUSE

This vacation house by architect Gunnar Berg, built for his family on the archipelago of Stockholm, consists of two independent structures resting on a common foundation — a planked wood "parterre." The roof is made of black asbestos sheets, from which metal chimneys protrude. The exterior walls are a collage of wooden door and window frames in various colors and sizes, joined to the wall surface by means of overhanging wood staves, and punctuated by the rhythm of vertical supporting elements, painted white.

The interior spaces are covered in polished wood planks and sheets of 1/8 in. (4 mm.) thick plywood. Two lofts at opposite ends of the main space contain sleeping areas which overlook the central living area. The services have been placed beneath the lofts. The living room is organized around the painted steel fireplace. The small secondary structure, with its sharply pitched roof, contains a small guest room and bath.

This is a successful example of an owner-built house, constructed with simple, semi finished materials, put together in clear, uncomplicated fashion. The interior has the feeling of a comfortable train in which the occupants are traveling about together.

Right: The small house built by architect/ owner Gunnar Berg. Simple, semi finished materials have been assembled in uncomplicated fashion in a collage of variously shaped windows and doors.

Above: Beneath the sloping roof are two sleeping lofts which face into the central space. The interior space is clad in sheets of 1/8 in. (4 mm.) thick plywood.

Below: A view from one of the two lofts. To the right is the sunken kitchen area.

Lower left: The central fireplace, of painted steel, is next to the entrance in the two-story living room.

Lower right: Old curved-wood Viennese chairs in the dining area.

COUNTRYSIDE

This old house in the countryside south of Copenhagen was built on a masonry foundation that supports a large wood roof covered in sod. The two gable walls are covered in vertical wood planks painted dark green.

A low, flat-roofed service area near the main house is used to accommodate guests. The two buildings, organized in an L-shape, enclose a small courtyard of smoothed down earth and paving stones. The interior spaces have been rebuilt and modernized by the owner, Jacob Asbaek, a sculptor and art dealer.

An intermediate floor has been left, with its wood beams and planks painted white. The center of the living area is taken up by a masonry chimney, adjacent to the kitchen area and the stairway to the attic. Floors are natural pine.

In the kitchen area the appliances are contained at the back of the masonry chimney structure and within the block of the counter. The walls of the living room are plaster. A functionalist tone pervades: the few furnishings are all white, including the small wicker tables. Along the walls, perfectly framed paintings echo the shape of the windows.

Above: The house is integrated into the natural setting. The sod roof brings the house into even closer harmony with the site.

Right: At the back, the central block contains the oven. Appliances are either fitted into the masonry wall or contained within the counter area.

Left: A principle of openly distributed space was put to work in the restoration of the house: the space of the ground floor is broken by the central block, which contains the traditional fireplace.

Below: In the living room the walls are white, as is the painted beam-and-plank ceiling. Chairs by Arne Jacobsen surround the dining table.

Above: An exterior view of the villa with the new wing housing the pool.

PORTICOED POOL

Architects Fritz and Josephine Pfaehler have modernized this large 1926 villa in Ulm in southern Germany. The house, situated within a forest area of tall trees, has four stories, the top one lying beneath the sloped roof. A stone foundation raises the structure above the ground.

The most noticeable element in the reconstruction is the addition of an indoor pool, enclosed within a two-story glass extension along one side of the building. The large window openings and the long outline of the blue pool, attached to the body of the old villa, act as a sort of portico, open to the lawn outside.

The rest of the work on the house was focused on redistribution of space, eliminating the small rooms and replacing them with ample, light-filled areas. The lower levels containing the living areas have large windows set in black enamel metal frames, silhouetted against the rough-finished white walls.

The upper floors hold work spaces and bedrooms; here the wooden structure of the sloping roof has been emphasized by exposing the beam work and filling in areas with chipboard, painted white.

Left: A corner of the second floor living room with the LC4 chair by Le Corbusier, designed in 1928 and manufactured by Cassina.

Left: The glassed-in "portals" that frame the ground floor pool.

Below: A view of the stairway leading to the upper floors.

Above: The bathroom beneath the sloping roof is equipped with modular storage units.

Left: The top floor study with the "Kevi" office chair, designed by J. Rasmussen.

ON THE ROCKS

Built in phases by architects Olli Kestilä and Eeva-Lüsa Salmi, this house rises above the smooth rocks of the Turku archipelago, in the gulf of Bothnia in Finland.

The building is grouped into two clusters, the smaller of the two for guests. The main building is organized around a large veranda, protected by the broad overhang of a gently sloping roof. A painted wood-plank terrace joins the two areas and then continues around the sides of the house to form a continuous exterior corridor. An approach of irregularly shaped paving stones separates the entrance from the surrounding low, dense vegetation. The specific arrangement of the two building areas and the unusual site of the house is conducive to summer outdoor living, when one can come into close contact with the flat expanse of the gulf landscape.

All the exterior walls are made of horizontal planks, painted and treated with the red, copper-rich earth of the area.

Natural wood is used on the interior, infusing it with warmth: tongue and groove on the ceiling and walls; long staves on the floor; large logs boxed together to create interior partitions.

The living area is dominated by the central fireplace made of brick and stone. A large stone slab has been fitted into the wooden floor directly in front of the fireplace.

All the objects within the house continue the warm, rural atmosphere: dry reeds in vases, the old-style coffee grinder on the wall, stones from the beach on the fireplace ledge, oil burning lamps. The simple, comfortable furnishings never call attention to themselves, but merge easily with the building itself.

The large openings in the outer walls are shielded by long, dark canvas curtains, which roll up. On the floor are smooth hand-woven rugs and a thick white fur in front of a built-in sofa.

Discreet and subdued, this house has a careful, respectful relationship between the inhabitants' activities and the natural setting.

Above: The veranda seen from the interior. During the summer this becomes the living room. In the background is the gulf of Bothnia which lies in the Baltic Sea.

Upper left: A view of the house carefully situated on the smooth rocks of the Turku archipelago.

Upper right: A view of the veranda showing the exterior paving stones.

Center: Two views of the terrace that joins the main bodies of the house.

Above: The summer living room: chairs and table were designed by Alvar Aalto between 1935 and 1939 and are manufactured by Artek.

Upper left: The living room with its large brick and stone fireplace. Rigorous attention to detail reinforces the subdued lines of the design.

Above: A view of the kitchen which opens onto the living room.

Above: Two details of the living room which occupies a large portion of the rectangular plan.

Above: During the day, sunlight from the ample windows fills the living room. The space is characterized by the use of wood for both construction and interior work, emphasizing a feeling of warmth and comfort. This is typical of this type of Scandinavian building, where structure and furnishings are successfully integrated into a formal unity. Furnishings are from the Korhonen factory.

REFUGE ON THE FJORD

Architect Nils Christie built this small vacation refuge that hugs the inaccessible shoreline of a fjord. It is surrounded by rocks worn smooth by the cold Norwegian water and by sparse trees and low shrubs, torn by the heavy winds.

Seen from the water, the house appears like a fortress on the high point of the shoreline. The volume of the house is compact, yet irregular and asymmetrical: one-half of the sloping roof covers the house in normal fashion; the other half opens up to reveal a portion of the floor below where the entrance lies. The walls are made of wide wood boards covered in black waterproof deck paint. Beneath the silvery line of the shiny metal eave, the brick chimney rises up from the fireplace, placed as is traditional, in the center of the living room.

The openings are irregular, depending upon the arrangement of the interior spaces. The tops of the tallest surrounding trees can be seen through the large windows.

Wood dominates in both the building and organization of the spaces and in the materials and tone of the furnishings.

The ground floor, with its ample windows, contains the living area, with the kitchen opening up toward the central brick fireplace. The furniture is handmade. The only valuable objects are the two Sigfrido chairs, carved and twisted with dragon-head arms, dramatically facing the entryway.

The wood floors were left unfinished and have darkened with use. On the ceiling, bolted structural beams, dropped storage areas, and curtain rods all intersect. The glass entrance corner is framed by a series of fixed windows, culminating in the triangular opening that follows the roof slope. In the kitchen the frame of the horizontal window extends inward, forming a niche and a ledge for various objects. The bedrooms lie on the upper floor; they are small, warm, alcovelike spaces.

Top: The house rises up on the rocks above the coast of a fjord. It is made completely of wood and has irregularly shaped windows arranged across the façade.

Center: Detail of a small space on the upper floor beneath the roof. Interior spaces are covered in smooth wood planks.

Below: A view from the dining area looking toward the kitchen with its built-in appliances, wall counter, and ceiling storage.

Right: The view from the living room. The dining table is attached to the wall beneath the window.

LIGHT AND GREEN SPACES IN THE CITY

LIGHT AND GREEN SPACES
IN THE CITY

ROOF TERRACE

Architects D. Cooper, M. Folonis, G. Elian, and R. Clemenson built this group of six attached dwellings in Santa Monica, California, a lovely residential area within metropolitan Los Angeles.

An eclectic design vocabulary emerges, tied to the complexity of the artificial Los Angeles landscape. This can be seen in the arrangement of the building elements, the frontal planes stepping backward as they move upward, and the gigantic colonnade of five towers. A feeling of spaciousness pervades. A short ramp leads to the cars in the basement. There, storage areas for the individual dwellings are next to the stairs which lead to a raised level from which the units overlook a common garden. The bedrooms are downstairs; the day zone is on the upper two levels, beneath an open roof terrace from which one can look out to sea. Upon entering any of the units, one passes into a two-story living room. A dining area is delineated by a curving wall which supports a loft that overlooks the living room. The loft leads directly up to the roof terrace. Behind the dining area are an open kitchen and a marine-style staircase leading to the mezzanine loft.

Left: Exterior view of the building punctuated by the stair towers.

Below: The open-plan kitchen behind the dining area. The marine-style stairs lead to the mezzanine.

Below: The mezzanine with its tubular iron railing; in the background, the stairs leading to the terrace.

Right: View of the mezzanine from the two-story living room. In the background, beneath the loft, the dining table and kitchen.
The dining area is arranged beneath the curved surface of the loft. The chairs are by Mies Van der Rohe, for Knoll, as is the tubular metal and leather armchair by Marcel Breuer.

GLASS FAÇADE

Richard and Su Rogers designed this single family house in Wimbledon, England, with a separate small apartment for guests and for a study. A broad garden separates the glass façade from the road, almost like a green noise-screen. The structure of the façade is defined by the iron beam spanning the single opening which is divided by the subtle vertical supports of the window frame — a legacy of the old International Style.

The building principles and formal choices adhere to the philosophy of recent English high-tech as espoused by Norman Foster or, as in this specific case, by Rogers, a designer of the Centre Pompidou, the Beaubourg, in Paris. Details are resolved in an efficient manner, hinging on a careful and subdued use of modules. The large living room is laid out with movable walls, a dropped ceiling with built-in lighting, and windows that extend the full height of the façade and are protected by full length shades — like something dreamed of by a disciple of Mies Van der Rohe.

A mirror screens off and hides the bedroom. The result, especially in the spaciously furnished interiors, is an epitome of the ideals of the Modern Movement: open spaces, light-filled, flexible, pure objects, spaciousness, horizontal painted backgrounds.

Prime examples of Modernist furniture complete the picture.

Left: The glass façade of the house facing onto the broad garden. The garden functions as a noise-screen and blocks off the main road.

Right: Detail of the recessed beam. The iron elements, painted yellow, mark the large entry façade.

Right: The mirrored wardrobe screens off the bedroom. In the background is the dining area.

Left: The dining room table and chairs are examples of an old Milanese design by Natan Roger.

Below: The large living room. The armchairs are Le Corbusier's LC1 and LC2 (manufactured by Cassina). The chair toward the back is by Marcel Breuer (manufactured by Knoll). To the left, stools by Alvar Aalto (manufactured by Artek).

WINTER GARDEN UNDER THE ROOF

Architects Alessandro Colbertaldo and Gianfranco Martelli have renovated and furnished this large attic space in the historic center of Novara, Italy. They have sensitively followed the purist tenets of the Modern Movement, translating them with scrupulous scholarship into a comfortable, workable design. A tall, narrow corridor forms an L-shape, skirting around the sleeping zone and leading directly into the large living area, which is trapezoidal in section. This space is ordered by a series of cruciform-shaped piers which separate an open area from one furnished with built-in pieces — a table, shelves, and a screen work — all of which evoke the luminous warmth of certain interiors by Le Corbusier. A sliding red metal partition separates a reading corner. The series of piers ends at a large sliding door where the volume of the room extends into the exterior loggia which is protected on the west by a sun-screen made of metal vertical slats. These frame a view of the dome of the church of San Gaudenzio by Antonelli and the 18th-century belltower of the Alfieri. Sunlight comes in through the sloping windows and the screened loggia. At the other end, the corridor ends in a similar space, paved in tile, containing a service area. In the corridor, as in the bedrooms, light filters in through the small glassed-in inner courts, open to the sky and filled with plants.

Right: Framed between the slats of the sun-screen is the dome of San Gaudenzio by Antonelli and the 18th-century belltower of the Alfieri.

Large photo: The large trapezoidal space receives light through the slanted windows and from the open screenwork of the loggia. In the background, Achille and Piergiacomo Castiglioni's "Arco" lamp, manufactured by Flos.

Above: The tiled corridor leads to the bedrooms. On the left, one of the inner courts.

Top right: One of the inner courts, filled with plants and open to the sky.

Left: A corner of the living room. The corridor ends in a space containing a low storage area. The cane and metal chairs are by Marcel Breuer, the sofas by Cassina.

REFLECTED LIGHT

Architect Paola Navone's Milan apartment ironically refuses to draw attention to itself. The design carefully focuses on what is absent, on empty spaces, on a poetic spareness and an appreciation of subtle, nearly negligible spaces, and on the reflection of light, sparkle, and the passage of time over objects and space.
The treatment of the walls and the choice of objects are evidence of a lively concern for decoration; there are shiny, colorful backgrounds and small spots of color imbued with great vitality.
The emphasis is on the unique quality of each space with its own special light and feeling. Empty areas are defined by objects which have been chosen for their decorative effect and their personal value: items brought back from trips, mementos, rather than chic up-to-the-minute possessions. The function of the various spaces is subtly expressed without fuss or self-consciousness: a corridor, an open room where plants turn toward the sun, an empty table, a small corner for cooking, a bed.
The spaces are clearly framed and defined by windows and old tile floors. The living room, with its shiny windows and walls, is full of plants.

Above: The bedroom with its large mosquito-net canopy.

Center: The only designer piece in the kitchen is the Bauhaus wall lamp. Everything else is either recycled or a prototype in development.

Right: Other than the many plants, the living room is nearly empty. The piece of furniture with a sliding front is a prototype by Paola Navone for Alchimia. The wall clock is Chinese.

Following page, left:
The corridor in Paola Navone's Milan apartment. The applique pieces on the wall brought back from China. In the background, the prototype for a lamp designed by Lapo Binazzi.

Following page, right:
The table floats in the empty room. The base is made up of elements from the Oikos system. The top is a sheet of the new Print Straticolor HPL.

IN AN OLD ORCHARD

Architect Gino Valle lives and works in a building complex in an area of Udine, Italy, which, when laid out in the Napoleonic era, contained orchards and religious institutions. Two of these three houses, renovated in collaboration with Piera Ricci Menichetti, are connected; the third lies beyond the garden. The core of the main building was built in the early 16th century; both a large one-story vaulted addition (with a terrace above) along the south façade and a small house in the garden were built in the 19th century. In 1930 another addition with services was built. There is no documentation on the house which is adjacent to the main structure, but it is old. This latter structure also contains three stories. When the architect began the renovation, in 1970, he took a free hand with the 1930 addition, restoring the house to some of its former spaciousness and light. He also connected the two separate buildings, joining them with a short flight of stairs. The interiors of both buildings have been retained as much as possible, including the original staircases. Wood partitions have been removed, and two new openings were made in the supporting walls. The original floors have been covered with seasoned elm. The studio takes up the ground floor as well as the small garden house. The living area is on the two upper floors.

Above left: The courtyard behind the house, on the site of the old orchard, is still a private, richly planted garden.

Second photo from top: The terrace area, opened up by the restoration work, has been paved in long planks.

Third photo from top: Interior spaces contain variously styled pieces of furniture: period pieces, designer pieces, and rustic furniture. This photo shows the second floor in front of the large terrace.

Lower left: The bookshelf by Ugo La Pietra in the long library space.

Above: A view toward the large terrace windows.

Left: The large tree-filled piazza looking toward the city. A red door to the studio and a blue door to the living area. The super-graphics on the white portico wall are by Carlo Ciussi.

Lower left: The stairs leading to the entrance to the living area. The small window looks into the living room.

Lower right: A view of the living room on the north side of the building.

ON THE COAST

This project by architect Nicola Pagliara consists of two separate apartments distributed over several floors. It is on the outskirts of town, at the top of the Cetara coast, overlooking the Bay of Amalfi, Italy.

Organic and elementary materials — cut stone, exposed cement, brick, primary colors — have been juxtaposed with a sense of the eclectic and the picturesque. The result is a stimulating, sensitive piece of architecture which relates both to Mediterranean culture and to the history and vocabulary of Rationalism, as well as to the idea of space and habitability of the great bourgeois villas. The fragmented façade, jagged with overhangs and projecting gutters, and the openings, ranging from minute to monumental (corresponding to the division of the interior spaces), evoke images of the military fortresses which dot the cliffs of the Mediterranean coast.

The interior also avoids a homogeneous design solution, juxtaposing powerful materials with a sensual division of space.

Above: Primary colors on organic and elementary materials make for strong dissonance between basic geometry and neo-baroque curves.

Lower left: Looking out on an angular terrace, a conversation area with Paolo Deganello's "Backbottom" chairs. On the terrace, a wheeled table by Enrico Baleri.

Lower right: The large porthole, cut diagonally into the stone wall. The "Frate" table and "Vela" chairs are by Enzo Mari. The "Arco" lamp is by Achille Castiglioni.

Opposite: The façade sited at the top of the Amalfi Coast.

Right: The dining area with a solar yellow concrete ceiling. The shelf-system on the left is "Minuetto" from the Oikos range; the round table "Astragalo", all designed by Antonia Astori De Ponti for Driade. The chairs "Delfina" were designed by Enzo Mari, the armchair and table "Sacher" by studio Sottsass Associati, all produced by Driade.

LIVING ROOM TERRACE

Architect Paolo Tommasi renovated this terrace at the top of an early 20th-century villa in Taormina, Sicily. The mild climate allows the terrace, which overlooks a park, to function as a living room.

The furnishings are like those for a sumptuous interior; they are protected by a lacquered screen, wood lined with stretched canvas. Track lighting has been installed, and the floor is covered with white ceramic tile. The furniture is made of lacquered metal.

The interior has a dropped ceiling with a square gridwork pattern, establishing continuity with the exterior. The furnishings, organized in functional groups, all follow square lines, including the soft pieces. The floor is covered with deep carpeting.

Interior and exterior, carefully unified, are suffused with subtle light from the surrounding landscape.

Above: The dining area. The dropped ceiling picks up the grid motif from the terrace. The bar in the corner is connected to the adjacent service zone. The "Edoardo" table and "Paolina" chair are by Paolo Tommasi.

Right: The terrace has ceramic floors and metal furniture designed by Paolo Tommasi. Benches, tables, and armchairs are placed beneath grillwork screened by horizontal shades of raw canvas. The surrounding landscape is the magnificent Taormina coast, in Sicily.

NATURAL MATERIALS

WOOD ART

Wood breathes, grows, changes, moves, ages; it emanates warmth and scents; it stirs up feelings. In their architectural treatises, Filarete and Francesco Di Giorgio have described the wood origins of architectural archetypes: "From the beginning nature furnished round columns of wood; subsequently, the practice arose, in certain places, of making these columns quadrangular."

Wood is the chosen material of Mario Ceroli, an artist who lives and works in Rome. His house, made from an old country shack, is also a museum for his artwork and furniture in wood. The ground floor of the three story building contains a studio/woodshop where the artist designs and executes his work; separate day and night zones are on the upper floors. Separated from the central body of the villa stands a small building, initially adapted as a studio and now transformed into a gallery/ warehouse. The striking stepped wood roof of this building is used as a stage for performances.

Playing on a delicate ambiguity between dwelling and museum, the villa proposes (albeit in a subtle fashion) what has become an increasingly accepted style — a house deriving its structure more from furniture and objects than from fixed building elements. This is design which has taken more from the theater than from a solid residential tradition. Here, the theater of performance and the theater of life merge; people move within ever-changing stage sets, with a sense of play, enjoyment, and experimentation.

Above: Exterior view of the villa made out of an old structure. Behind the wood framed windows, one can glimpse some of the artist's sculptures, such as the large multicolored rainbow.

Right: A large globe dominates the area around the house.

Opposite: A corner of the entrance where the focal point is the striking fireplace mask, sculpted by the artist. Ceroli has designed and signed all the furniture.

The façade of the house is topped by a single inclined plane, held up by wood brackets. The large windows are shielded by a low, rustic portico and an awning of curved terracotta tiles, supported by thin rough wood columns. Looking through the large windows, framed in natural wood, one can glimpse some of Ceroli's sculptures, such as the large multicolor rainbow. All the furniture is signed by the artist, some pieces built by hand, others industrially produced, but all made out of wood.

In the living room, near the large black grand piano, is a chimney wall which takes the form of an impressive carved mask. With its gaping eyes and mouth and its dilated nostrils, it evokes ancient Roman rituals.

Room after room is filled with sculpture, wall coverings, and furniture made of wood. The whole is exuberant, playful, diverting — a total work of art by Mario Ceroli.

Above: A view into the ground floor workshop with a sphinx made of layers of wood.

Below: View of the living room with a large wood chip painting on the wall.

Bottom center: The bathroom walls are covered in wood tiles; an obelisk and a de Chirico-derived chair dominate the space.

Bottom right: The living room seen from the artist's study. In the background the door leading to the studio/woodshop where Mario Ceroli creates his work. In the foreground, another globe.

Right: The living room seen through the large glass wall that opens onto a veranda. There is a pattern of fluid curved lines seen in the window wall and the interior arch leading to the next room, and repeated in the circular shape of the table in the center of the room.

TEXTILES

This New York loft, designed by Charles Forberg and Sam Takeuchi for Jack Lenor Larsen, the textile designer, is notable for its flexibility of space and function. The space flows freely, broken up only by the forms and colors of cushions, the soft furniture, the tapestries, and the simple Larsen textiles. Japanese-style rice-paper panels slide open to join together living and sleeping areas. There are five beds in this loft, but no bedroom, five eating areas but no dining room.

The loft area is a rectangle, about 23 ft. x 96 ft. (7 m. x 29 m.) divided into three large zones. The south end is an open, multifunctional space (living room, rest area, dining area) about 103 sq. ft. (96 sq. m.) in area. The central service zone, containing kitchen, bath, and other fixtures, is about 525 sq. ft. (49 sq. m.). The north end of the loft contains a 525 sq. ft. (49 sq. m.) studio, marked by a raised platform on which there is a large Japanese loom from Kyoto, used by Larsen to create his textiles.

Behind the loom, a small boxed-in pool of water reflects sunlight during the day, candlelight at night. The lowered vault ceiling is covered in brick; floors are done in pale ceramic tile.

Left: The south end of the loft, a multiuse space that opens onto a small loggia. To the right, a low Japanese table with tatami seating.

Right: Reverse view of the previous photo. Light comes in through a large opening in the ceiling.

Left: A view of the platform with the boxed-in pool. The floor is covered by one of Larsen's rugs. On the right, the walls between the windows are covered by mohair Swazi tapestries. In the foreground, small Japanese tables. In the background, an ivory-colored rice-paper panel. The lighting is by ceiling fixtures.

Water, sun, and greenery are the fundamental elements of Japanese residential tradition and ritual.

Right: View of the central corridor, toward Larsen's studio. The dividing walls of the service areas do not reach up to the full height of the loft, thus leaving the vaulted ceiling exposed and assuring ventilation throughout. Hanging on the walls are a variety of Oriental fishing nets and traps. A soft, colorful fabric hanging is draped from the ceiling. At the end of the corridor the loom from Kyoto is silhouetted against the light.

Left: The corridor connecting the multiuse space and studio. The service areas open up along the sides.

Center left: A sleeping loft, reached by a ladder, is above a closet.

Bottom left: A glass case filled with Japanese and African objects gathered during long trips to those parts of the world.

Right: A view of the main space looking toward the corridor. On the right, the open kitchen area. In the foreground, Alvar Aalto's famous tea cart.

Right: The living room. Sliding rice-paper panels reveal the glass cases along the walls where a collection of porcelain and glassware is kept.

Left: The Japanese Kawasaki loom (built in Kyoto) is on a raised platform in the studio at the extreme north end of the loft.

WOOD AND GLASS

The single family villa, recently built by Marco Zanuso in a beautiful part of the Lake Como, is a rare and successful example of Italian contemporary architecture in wood.
Natural materials have been used almost exclusively; only the underlying structure is steel. The house has an L-shaped plan, with two main sections enclosing a meadow that slopes down to a lake. Large sliding glass doors take the place of walls on two sides that open onto the meadow. The two long façades, looking toward the mountains, are covered entirely in red Canadian cedar shingles. These walls have only small windows for ventilation.
The short end walls have bay windows with thin metal frames.
On the interior, the parents' sleeping loft is reached by a separate stairway. The stairs that lead up to the children's sleeping loft may be raised and lowered by ropes. Kitchen, living room, dining area, and fireplace corner all form a unified space.

Right: Two views of the end walls of the villa covered in red Canadian cedar shingles. The bay windows are set within a bearing wall (below) and a small veranda. The structure was designed and engineered by Norbert Wackernell.

Bottom left: View of the corner between the two main units of the house, seen from the broad sloping meadow. The longer wall has large sliding glass doors.

Bottom right: A view of the living room. In the background, the kitchen with the cooking area in front. Toward the back, the tall block contains both kitchen sink and fireplace.

Opposite, above: A view of the living room from the kitchen counter. On the right, the dining area with a table by Zanuso. Above, the closed bulk of the parents' sleeping loft.

Opposite, below: Two details. On the left, the roof structure along the line of the gutter; on the right, the retractable stairway to the children's sleeping loft.

STONE

A young German artist has transformed these ancient stone and whitewashed structures into a residence and studio. The complex is in Santa Maria di Leuca at the extreme southern point of Puglia, Italy.

Set in a large valley crossed by a stream, the small group of buildings is surrounded by a wall of rough whitewashed stone. On one side, two small blocks accommodate the residence and the studio; these are flanked by a small oven and a stone and mud *tholos,* used for storage. There is a walled-in courtyard containing an outdoor kitchen covered by a tiled shed roof. The living area contains a large table and, leaning against the white plaster wall beneath the vaulted ceiling, a desk painted green. A handmade corner bench lies back to back against a painted wood wardrobe which, in turn, screens off the bed. The studio is almost completely filled by a ping-pong table, now used as a drawing table. Large rough wooden brackets and shelves leaning on sawhorses are attached to the unfinished walls.

Beyond the enclosing wall, far from the entrance and the opening into the courtyard, a low enclosure of stone and wood, barely rising above the ground, contains an area for animals, a well, and a small garden.

Above: Arriving from the fields, one first reaches the small complex to see the cutoff outline of the *tholos* warehouse.

Right: A general view of the complex and the two renovated straw barns. On the right, the whitewashed wood-burning oven; on the left, the edge of the garden/barnyard, with its well.

94

Left: The open air kitchen, seen from a corner of the courtyard. The top of the wood-burning oven is accessible by ladder. On the right one can see the table and bench used for outdoor dining. In the background, the bare, rolling landscape of Santa Maria di Leuca.

Above: A view of the interior courtyard. The open air kitchen is protected by a tiled shed roof, beneath which there are a small gas range and a sink. The pans are hung on the wall as is a small blue cabinet.

Opposite, above: A view of the living area with its dining table and painted desk. On the left, a corner seating area made from salvaged materials.

Opposite, below: Two other views of the living area, furnished with second-hand pieces, like the wardrobe, painted green. Behind the wardrobe is the bed, above which is the only window in the space.

CERAMICS, BRICK, AND WOOD

In the Venetian building tradition, practical knowledge of naval engineering has always been accompanied by a rare and subtle mastery of detail, an area which is usually the domain of painters and artisans. Thus, materials and technique are equally essential in the building of Venetian houses, ships, furniture, and paintings.

This splendid Venetian villa was built in the 17th century in Pozzolengo, near Mantua, Italy, when the area was still under Venetian rule. Modifications and additions continued to be made up until the beginning of this century; the present owners recently restored and repaired the building.

Today one large family lives in three separate areas of the villa. The two residential floors have been renovated with great care so that the large spaces, illuminated by tall windows, come alive with the colors and decorative motifs of the original materials. The architecture is complemented by a choice of simple but magnificent furnishings from the rural aristocratic tradition.

The handsome floors are covered in bricks of varied shapes and colors, horizontal wood strips or parquet inlays, and tiles. The many patterns and colors of these materials reveal the successive changes of four centuries of occupancy. The furnishings are few, leaving the emphasis on the tall proportions of the regular, symmetrical spaces. Placed beside the fireplace or the large windows, the sofas, armchairs, tables, and chairs appear almost out of scale, conveying a feeling of strangeness — a sense that this is not an ordinary residence.

Right: View of an addition surrounded by dense vegetation. Both the indoor and outdoor restoration has emphasized the original architectural and decorative elements.

Large photo, center: The music room, as in patrician palaces of old, is reserved for a single piano. The space is splendidly decorated with floor tiles.

Left: A view from the foyer looking toward the interior courtyard. In the background is an addition to the original house.

Right: Detail of addition surrounded by dense vegetation.

Below: The façade of the villa seen from the interior courtyard.

Lower right: A detail of the living room with its wood plank floor. A collection of Polish dolls is on the antique wood cart.

99

Above: The large kitchen with its beautiful masonry fireplace and walnut table. The floor is covered in square-cut earthenware tiles.

Right: The large indoor lemon garden on the upper floor. The decorations on the walls and ceiling are original.

Upper right: The large living room with the fireplace framed between two tall windows. The floor is covered in wood planks.

Right: The parents' bedroom is a large, light space, furnished with a few period pieces. The floor is covered in rectangular tiles.

BRICK AND GRANITE

Architect Ugo La Pietra has renovated the guest house on this working farm south of Milan. The 19th-century structure is adjacent to a farmhouse lived in by the people who work the land.

In the interior, large spaces are spread out over two levels. The barn, which was no longer needed for tobacco drying, has been converted into a broad portico which serves as an outdoor living room during the summer. The thick walls, the vaulted ceilings, and the brick arches and columns create an imposing series of spaces. The furnishings seem secondary — some pieces were already there and some were found on nearby farms and then restored. The brick floors are original in some spaces, new in others. The walls are exposed brick. The interior stairs linking the two floors of the building were built in a single long ramp between two brick walls, perforated by small holes containing lights.

Above: The house seen from the portico (formerly a barn). A large brick grill is used for outdoor cooking.

Above, three photos: Other views of the large ground floor space, the windows of which look out over a wide yard. Many of the objects have been collected from other regions of Italy. The drawers hanging on the wall in the center photo are from an herbalist's shop. In this, as in the other spaces in the house, the furniture comes from both the original building and from nearby farms. The ground floor also contains the kitchen and large dining room.

Large photo: The large ground floor space. Walls are varnished brick.

GLASS HOUSES
AND ALTERNATE ENERGY

BIO-HOUSE

This house, built by architects Rudolf Dörnach and Gerhard Heid on an isolated site outside Bonn, Germany, is a typical example of "bio-architecture," that is, a house powered by natural energy and built with materials taken directly from the surrounding area.

The entire structure is wood, except for the central supporting element in reinforced concrete. The outer walls are insulated with straw. The house has a hexagonal plan, elongated along the two sides of the main façade. The southwest side is completely closed in with a greenhouse wall. Heat is provided through a group of solar collector panels, placed outside the structure along the south side; these furnish hot water. The wind provides electricity via a large transmitter shaft on the roof connected to generators located in the 1290 sq. ft. (120 sq. m.) basement; the generators, in turn, feed into a series of batteries.

Right: A view of the house. On the right, the exterior collectors. The first floor of the house has an open plan comprising the living room and service areas. The sleeping zone is on the upper floor with the individual bedrooms arranged radially.

Below: A detail of the greenhouse behind the large window walls of the southwest façade. The greenhouse can be shaded by heavy black curtains, increasing the absorbant power of the energy.

Large photo: A view of the bio-house. An exterior stairway leads to the upper level. A wind generator on the top of the roof furnishes energy to the complex.

Below center: Another view of the greenhouse with large vases of flowers and vegetables.

Lower right: On the ground outside the house is a battery of solar collectors.

GREEN SOLAR ARCHITECTURE

In many ways, plants can be considered as solar energy converters through their process of photosynthesis. The close tie between the plant world and the sun is the underlying principle of "green solar architecture," a system proposed by a German research team which includes architects Dieter Schempp and Thomas Seidel. This experimental house in the countryside of Baden-Baden, Germany, exemplifies the most advanced research of its type, and is one of numerous projects built. The idea is to create a habitable space in close symbiosis with the plant world, integrating as much as possible all the energy potential offered by plants with that of the sun. In reality, the structure consists of a central greenhouse to which a traditional residential structure is attached in the back. Beyond the beneficial psychological effect of the man/plant symbiosis, the designers feel that this close contact between the inhabited space and the greenhouse interior markedly improved the quality of life in terms of both humidity and air temperature.

The filter of the greenhouse works as an efficient regulator of the air flow between the outside and the living zone, while maintaining a constant temperature and humidity level. However, to achieve these results, one has to pay close attention to combinations of plantings — not primarily for esthetic reasons, but rather to allow for uniformity of these natural "regulators." Thus items planted during one season will have time to develop during the following season, and so on.

Obviously, glass is the principal material in this design — not the traditional variety, but a technologically sophisticated, unbreakable type, designed to hold in heat and to insulate from noise.

Right: The experimental house in Baden-Baden, Germany. In front, the cascading glass wall of the greenhouse supported by a metal structure.

Right: The large greenhouse to which the sleeping zone is joined on an upper level. A system of curtains, suspended by weights from the inclined greenhouse roof, protects the interior spaces from the strong sunlight.

This integrated system allows consistent energy conservation, requiring only about 75% of the energy demanded by a conventional system. The house is set on a slope and consists of two distinct volumes enclosed within a third, that being the large greenhouse volume made of a glass screen supported by a metal structure. Beneath this cascade of glass, the two building units are like inhabited boxes, connected by walkways and railings.

Above: An exterior view of the greenhouse. To the right, below, a detail of the metal frame work holding up the large glass surfaces. There is unusual continuity between the dense, leafy landscape outside and the interior plantings, which appear somewhat lower, beneath the glass membrane.

Center, large photo: The upper level terrace facing into the greenhouse. The regular planking, the tubular iron, and the sun-shade grids clearly define the modularity of the prefabricated structure.

Extreme right, two photos: Above, walkways link the separate blocks that form the complex. Below, a view of the living room with its brick floor. The roof structure is exposed. Along the end wall a fixed window runs from floor to ceiling. Terrariums, pictures, and models add an educational dimension.

NURSERY GREENHOUSE

Several summers ago, Dieter Schempp, a German architect, transformed the interior of this nursery greenhouse into a residence and office. The greenhouse has continued to function as a place for plants. The designer has written: "Office signifies work, efficiency. One works and designs in an office, and so activity should be creative and should generate joy. But to think in this manner requires a brain functioning in the most open possible manner. Harmony between environment and individuals must be ensured as much as privacy and comfort. Why not then work in a natural setting? The greenhouse, natural setting *par excellence,* meets these requirements. As a place for working and for living it offers a stimulating variety of new impressions. Life within this 4300 sq. ft. (400 sq. m.) space has brought its occupants closer to nature; the confrontation, which has its own laws, has led them to develop new ways of thinking." The dining area has been placed within an interior walkway filled with plants. The office area is in the center of the space. Sunlight is screened off by colored curtains, drawn shut by cords which extend halfway down into the space. A plant research lab is located at the back of the structure. The kitchen is in the midst of growing plants. The sleeping zone is screened off by ample curtains.

Above: The sleeping zone screened off with ample curtains. The lamp behind the bed is the Tetrarch studio's "Pallade."

Center: The kitchen and dining area are surrounded by growing plants.

Below left: Another dining area set within the interior walkways.

Below center: The work table immersed within the greenery.

Below right: The colored fabric serves as a screen against the strong sunlight shining into the interior.

Right: The living room and dining area in a corner of the greenhouse/pavilion, near the entrance. The plants are less dense here.

GREENHOUSE TERRACE

The greenhouse has emerged as a distinct architectural type. Its principal requirements are of simplicity, maximum illumination, and a high level of thermal insulation for the interior space — all in order to artificially reproduce the conditions most favorable to the cultivation of exotic plants or to the production of various plant species. In its most elementary form the greenhouse requires little embellishment; any structure that is open to the sky can be transformed into a greenhouse with the simple addition of a glass roof.

The greenhouse terrace built by architects Del Greco and Grassi in Florence, Italy, is an example of this sort of project. It is a rectangular area, surrounded by walls of varying heights, some of them slanted. The preliminary plan was quite simple, calling for a terrace covered with a transparent roof, creating a greenhouse with veranda. Taking into account the slant of some of the parapets and the varying heights of the major perimeter walls, the designers created a roof that rises above the highest of the outer walls and is angled to the same degree as the major side walls.

Likewise, the metal structure supporting the glass panels is not perpendicular to the principal walls of the terrace. Along the plane of the roof it repeats the vertical slant. The result is a graphic play of lines silhouetted against the sky, grasping like hooks at the outside edges of the masonry structure.

Above: The greenhouse seen from above amid the rooftops of Florence.

Center: The parallel metal framework of the roof.

Below: Details of the greenhouse/terrace with the metal framework attached to the masonry structure.

Opposite, above: The greenhouse/terrace seen from the living area. The geometric patterns of the roof contrast with the regular shape of the plan.

Opposite, lower left: Detail of the long side with the masonry parapet.

Opposite, lower right: Interior corner detail.

SOLAR HOUSE

Architects Martin Schmidt and Martin Wagner built this small house in Bigorio, in the Italian section of Switzerland. It is set on a sloping, vineyard-covered hillside, where it is well exposed to the sun.

This is a composition that heeds the path of the sun, both in terms of equipment and spatial arrangements. Façades, windows, openings, and air flow all work together to define an innovative architectural form from the standpoint of energy and environment.

The composition focuses on the design of the south façade where large windows face the sun and where the roof is equipped with solar collectors.

The other façades are resolved with closed walls and small openings. The interior spaces are clear and precise, thought out, above all, in terms of their microclimate.

The project description reads: "...and so, for example, by leaving open the doors of the bedrooms, a light air flow is set up with the central space, making it possible to keep the windows closed and to conserve a great deal of energy." A greenhouse – a sort of winter garden – has been placed between the two main blocks of the structure which contain, respectively, the main residence and a small guest apartment.

Throughout, technical/industrial elements are emphasized, resulting in an expressive, poetic atmosphere.

Left: A surprising detail in the façade: one of the columns has been replaced by a cylindrical steel chimney.

Right: The greenhouse/winter garden between the two blocks of the building.

Above: The south façade of the house on the crest of the hill. The two story columns are silhouetted against the large window surfaces.

Left: Hi-tech elements have been emphasized.

Below: The roof is equipped with solar collectors.

Above, two photos:
The north face of the
house, illuminated by
subtle light sources,
opens inward. The
roof is glassed over.

Upper right: Stairs,
windows, openings —
all are carefully
planned to guarantee
optimum comfort
through the flow of
heat and air.

Right: In the kitchen
the traditional hood
has been replaced by
exposed stainless
steel pipes.

Opposite: The large,
central greenhouse
space is entirely
glassed in on the
south wall. During the
summer it can be
opened up and
shaded by a pergola.

MODULAR CONSTRUCTION

Architects Ritchie and Van den Bossche built this house in Fluy, a small village near Amiens in northern France. The entire front is open to a garden, thanks to a supporting steel structure with floor to ceiling sheets of glass, which surrounds the entire building. The modular structural elements employed by the designers/builders are noteworthy for their simple assembly. They took advantage of the natural slope of the loamy terrain and created a basement level which contains a wine cellar and solar energy storage.

As in all construction of this type, energy is conserved by combining the design with insulation and with mixed use of traditional and alternate energy sources. Radiant energy and reduced thermal dispersion have been emphasized by a sensible reduction in the heights of the interior spaces, by insulating the roof, by maintaining a constant temperature beneath the floors (made possible by the below ground service level), and by absorbing residual energy from the freezer, refrigerator, and lights directly into the heat distribution system.

The heating system is traditional oil, integrated, however, with a solar energy installation, decentralized over absorbant surfaces throughout the complex, according to the paths of the sun's rays during the day.

Right: The battery of solar panels arranged on the building's exterior.

Large photo: The south façade. The glass box covers a 2515 sq. ft. (234 sq. m.) surface, with only 150 sq. ft. (14 sq. m.) given over to living area. The structure was entirely prefabricated and assembled on site by two people working part-time over a ten month period.

WOOD AND WARMTH

This villa, built for a five-person family, lies on a small plot of land outside Cambridge, England. Only a long narrow stretch of the site was buildable, but the simple, economical design has taken advantage of this, extending outward in response to the terrain and opening on two sides to a garden. Architect David Thurlow used wood for both the exterior and interior walls in order to obtain good insulation and, consequently, to conserve energy.

The house contains ample common living areas and small bedrooms. The interior has been designed for possible changes in space allocations. Lighting the interior spaces was not a fundamental concern, making it possible to have two low, regularly shaped floors above ground. Nonetheless, the living zone benefits from the entire height of the building, due to the modest proportions of the bedrooms.

The ground floor contains the living room, dining room, kitchen, breakfast area, playroom, and services. The upper floor contains five bedrooms. The ground floor spaces face out, both onto a meadow, generally used for croquet games, and onto a more enclosed patio used as an outdoor living room.

Wood, one of the traditional materials of rural architecture, predominates in this house, both in the structure and in the details. This reinterprets a centuries-old but still applicable scheme, based on the rigorous and balanced proportions of the volumes. The furnishings and fixtures are simple and perfectly integrated with the architecture, allowing the purity of the spaces to prevail.

Above: The living room benefits from the full height of the building. In the background, the brick fireplace.

Center: The bathroom/dressing room, adjacent to the parents' bedroom.

Below: Across from the entrance, the kitchen faces out over a meadow.

Right: View of the ground floor space with the simple wooden staircase leading up to the night zone.

Left: The façade looking out over the meadow has two rows of windows, corresponding to the interior spaces on two floors. The opposite façade has a single line of large openings, corresponding to the ground floor spaces.

LIVING IN THE SUN

This small house belonging to a young German painter is in Ostuni, in Southern Italy, a whitewashed village oriented to the sun. In hot, southern Mediterranean regions, the architecture of entire cities seems locked into close accord with the sun: the white protective walls; the narrow, cool streets; the few but indispensable tiny windows; and, of course, the sun, everpresent, concentrated and luminous. This little house is very simple. It consists of a single large vaulted space, opening onto a narrow pedestrian street, and a lovely little rear balcony looking out over the landscape. A tiny bathroom is at the top of a staircase; a kitchen is reached by going down a few steps. The sparse furniture is secondhand.

To enter one must go down a few stone steps. A large table, used for work and for dining, is in the center of the room. Just a few feet away is an iron bed, also placed toward the center of the room, away from the wall. A chest and an imposing wood credenza are placed against the two blank walls.

The small kitchen has a little window that opens onto the balcony. The window, the balcony, and the door are the only openings in the space.

Right: The small residence as seen from the kitchen which lies below the pink stone steps.

Large photo: A general view. To enter, one goes down a few stone steps.

Above: A typical street in Ostuni. The houses, stacked one against the other, form white blocks joined by steep, narrow passageways.

Left: The small kitchen has a window opening onto a balcony.

Center: In Ostuni the doors of houses open directly onto the street.

Left: Detail of the small balcony. It is inviting, despite its small size due to location of the house in the upper part of the town.

Below: A general view of Ostuni in Puglia.